Sleep, Baby, Sleep

Sleep, Baby, Sleep

LULLABIES AND NIGHT POEMS

Selected and Illustrated by

MICHAEL HAGUE 98-11760

Morrow Junior Books

NEW YORK

To Lovey the Lion and his little girl

"The White Seal's Lullaby" melody line © 1965 by Alec Wilder and William Envick, reprinted by permission of HarperCollins Publishers. "Dear Father" © 1943 by Margaret Wise Brown, reprinted by permission of HarperCollins Publishers. "Good Night" © 1980 by Nikki Giovanni, from *Vacation Time* by Nikki Giovanni, reprinted by permission of William Morrow and Co., Inc. "Lullaby" © 1988 by John Plotz, reprinted by permission of the author. "Sleep, Sleep, Sleep" © 1988 by Elizabeth Shub, from *A Week of Lullabies* by Helen Plotz, reprinted by permission of the author. "What Happens to the Colors?" © 1985 by Jack Prelutsky, from *My Parents Think I'm Sleeping* by Jack Prelutsky, reprinted by permission of Greenwillow Books, a division of William Morrow and Co., Inc. "A Christmas Lullaby" by Margaret Hillert, used by permission of the author, who controls all rights.

Printed in the United States of America
Designed by Marc Cheshire
1   3   5   7   9   10   8   6   4   2

Library of Congress Cataloging-in-Publication Data
Sleep, baby, sleep: lullabies and night poems/selected by Michael Hague:
illustrated by Michael Hague.   p.   cm.
ISBN 0-688-10877-6
1. Children's poetry.   2. Lullabies.   [1. Poetry Collections.   2. Bedtime—Poetry.   3. Sleep—
Poetry.   4. Night—Poetry.   5. Lullabies.]   I. Hague, Michael.   PN6109.97.S58   1994
808.81'0083—dc20   93-27119   CIP   AC

CONTENTS

LULLABIES

Lullaby and Good Night

Lullaby and good night, with roses bedight,
With lilies bedecked, is baby's wee bed.
Lay thee down now and rest, may thy slumber be blest,
Lay thee down now and rest, may thy slumber be blest.

JOHANNES BRAHMS

Sleep, Little Child

Sleep, little child, go to sleep,
Mother is here by your bed.
Sleep, little child, go to sleep,
Rest on the pillow your head.

The world is silent and still,
The moon shines bright on the hill,
And creeps past your windowsill.

Sleep, little child, go to sleep,
Go to sleep, go to sleep.

Lavender's Blue

Lavender's blue, dilly, dilly,
Lavender's green,
When I am king, dilly, dilly,
You shall be queen.

Call up your men, dilly, dilly,
Set them to work,
Some to the plough, dilly, dilly,
Some to the cart.

Some to make hay, dilly, dilly,
Some to cut corn,
While you and I, dilly, dilly,
Keep out of harm.

Bye, Baby Bunting

Bye, baby bunting,
Father's gone a-hunting,
Mother's gone a-milking,
Sister's gone a-silking,
Brother's gone to buy a skin
To wrap the baby bunting in.

Golden Slumbers

Golden slumbers kiss your eyes;
Smiles await you when you rise;
Sleep, pretty baby, do not cry,
And I will sing a lullaby.

Care you know not, therefore sleep,
While I o'er you watch do keep.
Sleep, pretty baby, do not cry,
And I will sing a lullaby.

THOMAS DEKKER

Twinkle, Twinkle, Little Star

Twinkle, twinkle, little star,
How I wonder what you are.
Up above the world so high,
Like a diamond in the sky.
Twinkle, twinkle, little star,
How I wonder what you are!

JANE TAYLOR

All the Pretty Little Horses

Hushabye, don't you cry,
Go to sleepy, little baby;
When you wake, you shall have cake,
And all the pretty little horses,
Black and bay, dapple and gray,
Coach and six white horses.
All the pretty little horses.

All Through the Night

Sleep, my child, and peace attend thee,
All through the night;
Guardian angels God will send thee,
All through the night;
Soft the drowsy hours are creeping,
Hill and vale in slumber sleeping,
I my loving vigil keeping,
All through the night.

Hush, Little Baby

Hush, little baby, don't say a word,
Papa's going to buy you a mockingbird.
And if that mockingbird won't sing,
Papa's going to buy you a diamond ring.
If that diamond ring turns brass,
Papa's going to buy you a looking glass.

If that looking glass gets broke,
Papa's going to buy you a billy goat.
If that billy goat won't pull,
Papa's going to buy you a cart and bull.
If that cart and bull turns over,
Papa's going to buy you a dog named Rover.
If that dog named Rover won't bark,
Papa's going to buy you a horse and cart.
If that horse and cart fall down,
You'll still be the sweetest baby in town!

Rockabye, Baby

Rockabye, baby, on the tree top,
When the wind blows, the cradle will rock;
When the bough breaks, the cradle will fall,
And down will come baby, cradle and all.

Little Boy Blue

Little Boy Blue, come blow your horn,
The sheep's in the meadow, the cow's in the corn.
Where is the boy who looks after the sheep?
He's under the haystack fast asleep.

Sweet and Low

Sweet and low, sweet and low,
Wind of the western sea,
Low, low, breathe and blow,
Wind of the western sea!
Over the rolling waters go,
Come from the dying moon, and blow,
Blow him again to me
While my little one, while my pretty one
Sleeps.

Sleep and rest, sleep and rest,
Father will come to thee soon;
Rest, rest, on mother's breast,
Father will come to thee soon;
Father will come to his babe in the nest,
Silver sails all out of the west
Under the silver moon.
Sleep, my little one, sleep, my pretty one,
Sleep.

ALFRED, LORD TENNYSON

Now the Day Is Over

Now the day is over,
Night is drawing nigh,
Shadows of the evening,
Steal across the sky.

Now the darkness gathers,
Stars begin to peep,
Birds and beasts and flowers
Soon will be asleep.

SABINE BARING-GOULD

Raisins and Almonds

To my little one's cradle in the night,
Comes a little goat snowy and white.
The goat will trot to the market,
While mother her watch does keep,
Bringing back raisins and almonds.
Sleep, my little one, sleep.

Dance to Your Daddy

Dance to your daddy, my little laddie,
Dance to your daddy, my little lamb.
You shall have a fishy on a little dishy,
You shall have a fishy when the boat comes in.
Dance to your daddy, my little laddie,
Dance to your daddy, my little lamb.

Wee Willie Winkie

Wee Willie Winkie runs through the town,
Upstairs and downstairs in his nightgown,
Rapping at the window,
crying through the lock,
"Are the children in their beds,
For now it's eight o'clock?"

Sleep, Baby, Sleep

Sleep, baby, sleep,
Thy father guards the sheep.
Thy mother shakes the dreamland tree,
And from it fall sweet dreams for thee.
Sleep, baby, sleep,
Sleep, baby, sleep.

The Fairyship

I saw a ship a-sailing,
A-sailing on the sea;
And O! it was all laden
With pretty things for thee!

There were comfits in the cabin
And apples in the hold;
The sails were made of silk,
And the masts were made of gold!

The four and twenty sailors
That stood between the decks
Were four and twenty white mice
With chains about their necks.

The captain was a duck,
With a packet on his back;
And when the ship began to move,
The captain said, "Quack! Quack!"

Father, We Thank Thee

Father, we thank Thee for the night,
And for the pleasant morning light,
For rest and food and loving care,
And all that makes the world so fair.

Help us to do the things we should,
To be to others kind and good,
In all we do, in all we say,
To grow more loving every day.

Suo Gan

Sleep, my baby, on my bosom,
Warm and cozy it will prove;
Round thee mother's arms are folding,
In her heart a mother's love.
There shall no one come to harm thee,
Naught shall ever break thy rest.
Sleep my darling babe in quiet,
Sleep on mother's gentle breast.

The Sandman

The flowers are sleeping
Beneath the moon's soft light,
With heads close together
They dream through the night.
And leafy trees rock to and fro
And whisper low—
Sleep, sleep, lullaby,
O sleep, my darling child.

Now birds that sang sweetly,
To greet the morning sun,
In little nests are sleeping
Now twilight has begun.
The cricket chirps its sleepy song,
Its dreamy song—
Sleep, sleep, lullaby,
O sleep, my darling child.

The Sandman comes on tiptoe
And through the window peeps,
To see if little children
Are in their beds asleep.
And when a little child he finds
Casts sand in his eyes—
Sleep, sleep, lullaby,
O sleep, my darling child.

JOHANNES BRAHMS

Hey Diddle Diddle

Hey diddle diddle,
The cat and the fiddle,
The cow jumped over the moon.
The little dog laughed to see such sport,
And the dish ran away with the spoon.

The White Seal's Lullaby

Oh! hush thee, my baby, the night is behind us,
And black are the waters that sparkled so green.
The moon, o'er the combers, looks downward to find us
At rest in the hollows that rustle between.
Where billow meets billow, there soft be thy pillow,
Oh, weary wee flipperling, curl at thy ease!
The storm shall not wake thee, nor shark overtake thee,
Asleep in the arms of the slow-swinging seas.

RUDYARD KIPLING

When at Night I Go to Sleep

Sandman is here!
Let us first say our evening prayer!
When at night I go to sleep,
Fourteen angels watch do keep;
Two my head are guarding,
Two my feet are guiding,
Two are on my right hand,
Two are on my left hand,
Two who warmly cover,
Two who o'er me hover,
Two to whom 'tis given
To guide my steps to Heaven.

ENGELBERT HUMPERDINCK

Oh, How Lovely Is the Evening

Oh, how lovely is the evening,
Is the evening,
When the bells are sweetly ringing,
Sweetly ringing,
Ding, dong, ding, dong, ding, dong.

The Sandman Comes

The Sandman comes, the Sandman comes,
He brings such pretty snow-white sand.
For ev'ry child throughout the land,
The Sandman comes.

NIGHT POEMS

Day Is Done

Day is done,
Gone the sun—
From the earth,
From the hills,
From the sky.
All is well,
Safely rest.
God is nigh.

Dear Father

Dear Father,
Hear and bless
Thy beasts and
Singing birds,
And guard with
Tenderness
Small things
That have
No words.

MARGARET WISE BROWN

Now I Lay Me Down to Sleep

Now I lay me down to sleep,
I pray thee, Lord, my soul to keep;
Thy love go with me all the night
And wake me with the morning light.

Safe in Bed

Matthew, Mark, Luke and John,
Bless the bed I lie on!
Four corners to my bed,
Five angels there lie spread:
   Two at my head,
   Two at my feet,
One at my heart, my soul to keep.

I See the Moon

I see the moon,
And the moon sees me;
God bless the moon,
And God bless me.

Star Light, Star Bright

Star light, star bright,
First star I see tonight,
I wish I may, I wish I might,
Have the wish I wish tonight.

My Bed Is a Boat

My bed is like a little boat;
Nurse helps me in when I embark;
She girds me in my sailor's coat
And starts me in the dark.

At night, I go on board and say
Good night to all my friends on shore;
I shut my eyes and sail away
And see and hear no more.

And sometimes things to bed I take,
As prudent sailors have to do;
Perhaps a slice of wedding cake,
Perhaps a toy or two.

All night across the dark we steer;
But when the day returns at last,
Safe in my room, beside the pier,
I find my vessel fast.

ROBERT LOUIS STEVENSON

Hushabye Baby

Hushabye baby,
Thy cradle is green,
Father's a nobleman,
Mother's a queen.
Betty's a lady
And wears a gold ring,
John is a drummer
And drums for the king.
Boom-tiddy, boom-tiddy,
Boom, boom, boom.

Good Night to My Babe

Good night to my babe and sweet be your sleep.
May silence enfold you, your slumber be deep.
Good night, good night, good night, good night.

Good Night

Little baby, lay your head
On your pretty cradle-bed;
Shut your eye-peeps, now the day
And the light are gone away;
All the clothes are tucked in tight;
Little baby dear, good night.

Yes, my darling, well I know
How the bitter wind doth blow;
And the winter's snow and rain
Patter on the windowpane;
But they cannot come in here,
To my little baby dear;

For the window shutteth fast,
Till the stormy night is past;
And the curtains warm are spread
Round about her cradle-bed.
So till morning shineth bright,
Little baby dear, good night.

JANE TAYLOR

Tree Shadows

All hushed the trees are waiting
On tiptoe for the sight
Of moonrise shedding splendor
Across the dusk of night.
Ah, now the moon is risen
And lo, without a sound
The trees all write their welcome
Far along the ground!

Night

The sun descending in the west
The evening star does shine;
The birds are silent in their nest,
And I must seek for mine.

The moon like a flower
In heaven's high bower,
With silent delight,
Sits and smiles on the night.

WILLIAM BLAKE

Little One, My Baby

Little one, my baby, little one, my heart!
Little one, my joy, and little one, my love!
Sleep now! Sleep now!
Little one, my child, who won't go to sleep,
Time to go to sleep, time to go to sleep.
Sleep now! Sleep now!

How They Sleep

Some things go to sleep in such a funny way:
Little birds stand on one leg and tuck their heads away.
Chickens do the same, standing on their perch;
Little mice lie soft and still as if they were in church.
Kittens curl up close, in such a funny ball;
Horses hang their sleepy heads and stand still in a stall.

Sometimes dogs stretch out or curl up in a heap;
Cows lie down upon their sides when they go to sleep.
But little babies dear are snugly tucked in beds,
Warm with blankets, all so soft, and pillows for their heads.
Bird and beast and babe—I wonder which of all—
Dream the dearest dreams that down from dreamland fall!

The Land of Nod

From breakfast on all through the day
At home among my friends I stay;
But every night I go abroad
Afar into the land of Nod.

All by myself I go,
With none to tell me what to do—
All alone beside the streams
And up the mountainsides of dreams.

The strangest things are there for me,
Both things to eat and things to see,
And many frightening sights abroad
Till morning in the land of Nod.

Try as I like to find the way,
I never can get back by day,
Nor can remember plain and clear
The curious music that I hear.

ROBERT LOUIS STEVENSON

At Night

When I go to bed at night,
The darkness is a bear.
He crouches in the corner
Or hides behind a chair;
The one who tells me stories—
She does not know he's there.

But when she kisses me good night,
And darkness starts to creep
Across the floor, why, then I see
It's just a woolly sheep
That nibbles at my rugs awhile
Before we go to sleep.

ANNE BLACKWELL PAYNE

Lullaby, Oh Lullaby!

Lullaby, oh lullaby!
Flowers are closed and lambs are sleeping,
Lullaby, oh lullaby!
Stars are up, the moon is peeping;
Lullaby, oh lullaby!
While the birds are silence keeping,
(Lullaby, oh lullaby!)
Sleep, my baby, fall a-sleeping,
Lullaby, oh lullaby!

CHRISTINA ROSSETTI

All the World Is Sleeping

Go to sleep upon my breast,
All the world is sleeping.
Till the morning's light you'll rest,
Mother watch is keeping.

Birds and beasts have closed their eyes,
All the world is sleeping.
In the morn the sun will rise,
Mother watch is keeping.

Good Night

Good night Mommy
Good night Dad

I kiss them as I go

Good night Teddy
Good night Spot

The moonbeams call me so

I climb the stairs
Go down the hall
And walk into my room

My day of play is ending
But my night of sleep's in bloom

NIKKI GIOVANNI

A Chill

What can lambkins do
All the keen night through?
Nestle by their woolly mother,
The careful ewe.

What can nestlings do
In the nightly dew?
Sleep beneath their mother's wing
Till day breaks anew.

If in field or tree,
There might only be
Such a warm soft sleepy place
Found for me!

CHRISTINA ROSSETTI

Lullaby

Cat's in the alley
Flower's in the pot
Moon's in the sky and
Baby's in the cot

Tree and the lamppost
Standing by the door
Big dog is sleeping
On the kitchen floor

Now nighttime is falling
There are shadows all around
Baby's gonna sleep
Till the sun shines down

Mama and Papa
Are standing by your bed
Sweet dreams are coming
To fill your sleepy head

JOHN PLOTZ

Sleep, Sleep, Sleep

Sleep, sleep, sleep
Father's gone to town
What will he bring? A loaf of bread
God bless baby's head

Sleep, sleep, sleep
Father's gone to town
What will he bring? Two cherry pies
God bless baby's eyes

Sleep, sleep, sleep
Father's gone to town
What will he bring? A woolen vest
God bless baby's chest

Sleep, sleep, sleep
Father's gone to town
What will he bring? Three silver charms
God bless baby's arms

Sleep, sleep, sleep
Father's gone to town
What will he bring? A special treat
God bless baby's feet

Sleep, sleep, sleep

ADAPTED BY ELIZABETH SHUB

Winkum, Winkum

Winkum, winkum, shut your eye
Sweet my baby, lullaby.
For the dews are falling soft,
Lights are flickering up aloft;
And the moonlight's peeping over
Yonder hilltop capped with clover.

Chickens long have gone to rest,
Birds lie snug within their nest.
And my birdie soon will be
Sleeping like a chickadee.
For with only half a try
Winkum, winkum, shuts her eye.

What Happens to the Colors?

What happens to the colors
When night replaces day?
What turns the wrens to ravens,
The trees to shades of gray?

Who paints away the garden
When the sky's a sea of ink?
Who robs the sleeping flowers
Of their purple and their pink?

What makes the midnight clover
Quiver black upon the lawn?
What happens to the colors?
What brings them back at dawn?

JACK PRELUTSKY

A Christmas Lullaby

Hushabye, rockabye, softly to sleep,
Soft as the snow that is drifting and blowing.
Hushabye, rockabye, shadows are deep
Blue on the snow that is endlessly snowing.
Sleep like the animals sleepily curled
In soft little nests in a winter white world.
Hushabye, rockabye, till the stars creep
Into a day that is shining and glowing.

MARGARET HILLERT

MUSICAL
ARRANGEMENTS

Lullaby and Good Night

Johannes Brahms

Lul-la-by and good night, with roses be-dight,— With
lil-ies be-decked, is baby's wee bed. Lay thee
down now and rest, may thy slum-ber be blest,— Lay thee
down now and rest, may thy slum-ber be blest.

Sleep, Little Child

Sleep, lit-tle child, go to sleep, Moth-er is here by your
bed. Sleep, lit-tle child, go to sleep, Rest on the pil-low your
head.— The world is si-lent and still,— The moon shines bright on the
hill,— And creeps past your win-dow-sill. Sleep, lit-tle child, go to
sleep,— Go to sleep,— go to sleep.

Lavender's Blue

La - ven - der's blue, dil - ly, dil - ly, La - ven - der's green,

When I am king, dil - ly, dil - ly, You shall be queen.

Call up your men, dilly, dilly,
Set them to work,
Some to the plough, dilly, dilly,
Some to the cart.

Some to make hay, dilly, dilly,
Some to cut corn,
While you and I, dilly, dilly,
Keep out of harm.

Golden Slumbers

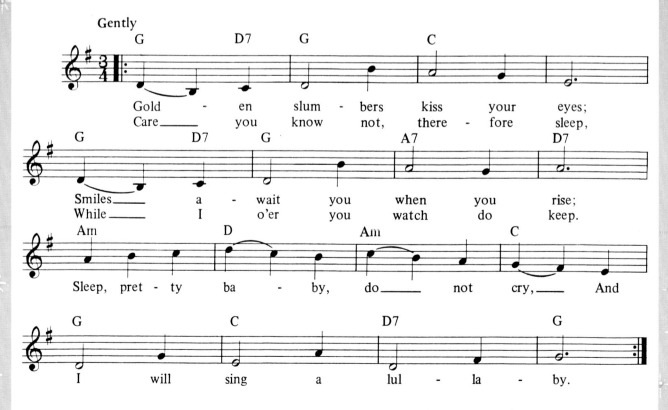

Gold - en slum - bers kiss your eyes;
Care___ you know not, there - fore sleep,

Smiles___ a - wait you when you rise;
While___ I o'er you watch do keep.

Sleep, pret - ty ba - by, do___ not cry,___ And

I will sing a lul - la - by.

Bye, Baby Bunting

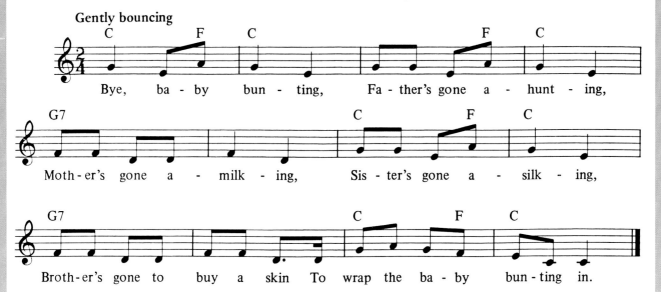

Bye, ba-by bun-ting, Fa-ther's gone a - hunt-ing,

Moth-er's gone a - milk-ing, Sis-ter's gone a - silk-ing,

Broth-er's gone to buy a skin To wrap the ba-by bun-ting in.

Twinkle, Twinkle, Little Star

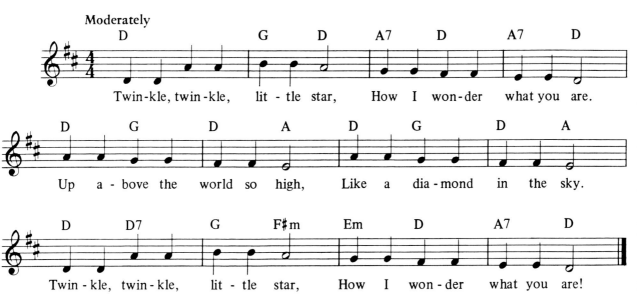

Twin-kle, twin-kle, lit-tle star, How I won-der what you are.

Up a - bove the world so high, Like a dia-mond in the sky.

Twin-kle, twin-kle, lit-tle star, How I won-der what you are!

All the Pretty Little Horses

Softly

Hush - a - bye, don't you cry, Go to sleep-y, lit - tle ba - by; When you wake, you shall have cake, And all the pret-ty lit - tle hors - es, Black and bay, dap - ple and gray, Coach and six___ white___ hors - es. All the pret - ty lit - tle hors - es.

All Through the Night

Slowly

Sleep, my child, and peace at - tend thee, All through the night; Guard - ian an - gels God will send thee, All through the night; Soft the drow - sy hours are creep - ing, Hill and vale in slum - ber sleep - ing, I my lov - ing vig - il keep - ing, All through the night.

68

Hush, Little Baby

If that billy goat won't pull,
Papa's going to buy you a cart and bull.
If that cart and bull turns over,
Papa's going to buy you a dog named Rover.
If that dog named Rover won't bark,
Papa's going to buy you a horse and cart.
If that horse and cart fall down,
You'll still be the sweetest baby in town!

Rockabye, Baby

Gently rocking

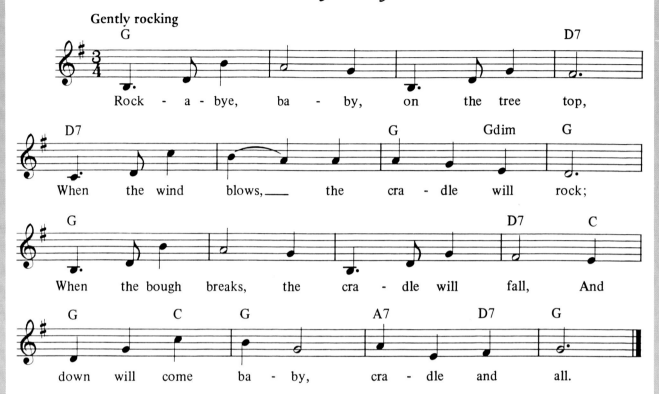

Rock - a - bye, ba - by, on the tree top,
When the wind blows, ___ the cra - dle will rock;
When the bough breaks, the cra - dle will fall, And
down will come ba - by, cra - dle and all.

Little Boy Blue

With a slight lift

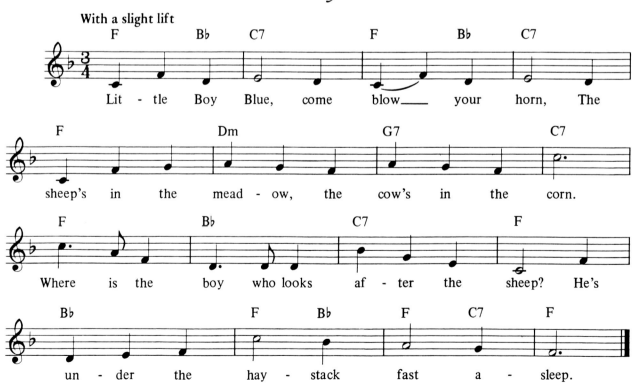

Lit - tle Boy Blue, come blow ___ your horn, The
sheep's in the mead - ow, the cow's in the corn.
Where is the boy who looks af - ter the sheep? He's
un - der the hay - stack fast a - sleep.

Sweet and Low

Gently flowing

Sweet and low, sweet and low, Wind of the west - ern sea,_____ Low, low, breathe and blow, Wind of the west - ern sea!_____ O - ver the roll - ing wa - ters go, Come from the dy - ing moon,_ and blow, Blow him a - gain to me_____ While my lit - tle one, while my pret - ty one sleeps.

Sleep and rest, sleep and rest,
Father will come to thee soon;
Rest, rest, on mother's breast,
Father will come to thee soon;
Father will come to his babe in the nest,
Silver sails all out of the west
Under the silver moon.
Sleep, my little one, sleep, my pretty one,
Sleep.

Now the Day Is Over

Sabine Baring-Gould   *Joseph Barnby*

Now the day is__ o-ver, Night is draw-ing__ nigh,__

Shad-ows of the eve-ning, Steal a-cross the sky.

Now the darkness gathers,
Stars begin to peep,
Birds and beasts and flowers
Soon will be asleep.

Raisins and Almonds

With warmth

To my lit-tle one's cra-dle in the night,__ Comes a

lit-tle goat snow-y and__ white.__ The

goat will trot to the mar-ket,__ While moth-er her watch__ does

keep,__ Bring-ing back rai-sins and al-monds.__

Sleep, my lit-tle one, sleep.__

Dance to Your Daddy

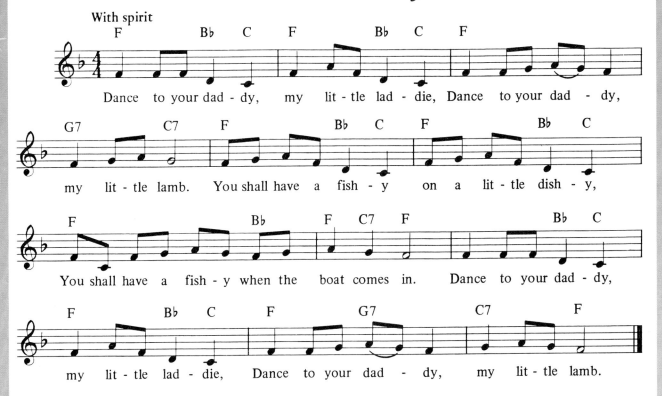

With spirit

Dance to your dad - dy, my lit - tle lad - die, Dance to your dad - dy, my lit - tle lamb. You shall have a fish - y on a lit - tle dish - y, You shall have a fish - y when the boat comes in. Dance to your dad - dy, my lit - tle lad - die, Dance to your dad - dy, my lit - tle lamb.

Wee Willie Winkie

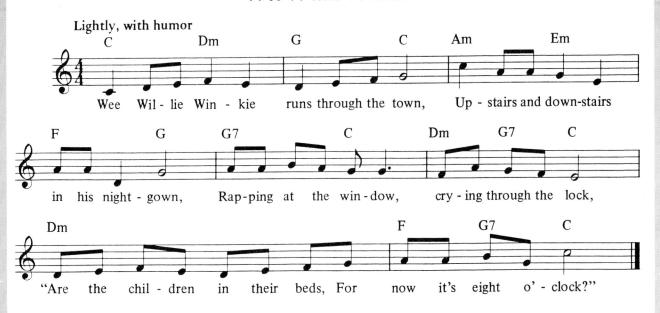

Lightly, with humor

Wee Wil - lie Win - kie runs through the town, Up - stairs and down-stairs in his night - gown, Rap-ping at the win - dow, cry - ing through the lock, "Are the chil - dren in their beds, For now it's eight o' - clock?"

Sleep, Baby, Sleep

Softly

Sleep, ba - by, sleep, Thy fa - ther guards the sheep. Thy moth - er shakes the dream - land tree, And from it fall sweet dreams for thee. Sleep, ba - by, sleep, Sleep, ba - by, sleep.

Father, We Thank Thee

With feeling

Fa - ther, we thank Thee for___ the___ night, And for the pleas - ant morn - ing___ light, For rest and food and lov - ing___ care, And all that makes the___ world so___ fair.

Help us to do the things we should,
To be to others kind and good,
In all we do, in all we say,
To grow more loving every day.

74

The Fairyship

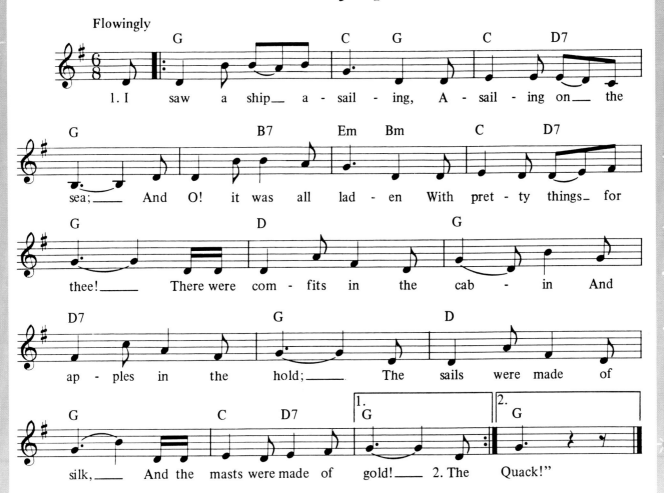

Flowingly

1. I saw a ship a-sail-ing, A-sail-ing on the sea; And O! it was all lad-en With pret-ty things for thee! There were com-fits in the cab-in And ap-ples in the hold; The sails were made of silk, And the masts were made of gold! 2. The Quack!"

2. The four and twenty sailors
That stood between the decks
Were four and twenty white mice
With chains about their necks.

The captain was a duck,
With a packet on his back;
And when the ship began to move,
The captain said, "Quack! Quack!"

Suo Gan

The Sandman

Johannes Brahms

2. Now birds that sang sweetly,
   To greet the morning sun,
   In little nests are sleeping
   Now twilight has begun.
   The cricket chirps its sleepy song,
   Its dreamy song—
   Sleep, sleep, lullaby,
   O sleep, my darling child.

3. The Sandman comes on tiptoe
   And through the window peeps,
   To see if little children
   Are in their beds asleep.
   And when a little child he finds
   Casts sand in his eyes—
   Sleep, sleep, lullaby,
   O sleep, my darling child.

Hey Diddle Diddle

Hey did - dle did - dle, The cat and the fid - dle, The
cow jumped o - ver the moon.___ The lit - tle dog laughed_ to
see such sport, And the dish ran a - way with the spoon._____

Oh, How Lovely Is the Evening

Oh, how love - ly is the eve - ning,
Is the eve - ning, When the bells are
sweet - ly ring - ing, Sweet - ly ring - ing, Ding,
dong, ding, dong, ding, dong.

The White Seal's Lullaby

Rudyard Kipling   *Alec Wilder*

Reassuringly

Oh! hush thee, my ba – by, the night is be – hind us, And
black are the wa – ters that spar – kled so green. The
moon, o'er the comb – ers, looks down – ward to find us At
rest in the hol – lows that rus – tle be – tween. Where
bil – low meets bil – low, there soft be thy pil – low, Oh,
wea – ry wee flip – per – ling, curl at thy ease! The
storm shall not wake thee, nor shark o – ver – take thee, A –
sleep in the arms of the slow – swing – ing seas.

When at Night I Go to Sleep

Engelbert Humperdinck

Flowingly, with feeling

Sand-man is here! Let us first say our eve - ning prayer!

When at night I go to sleep, Four - teen an - gels watch do— keep;

Two my head are guard - ing, Two my feet are guid - ing,

Two are on my right hand, Two are on my left hand,

Two who warm - ly cov - er, Two who o'er me hov - er,

Two to whom 'tis giv - en To guide my steps to Heav - en.

The Sandman Comes

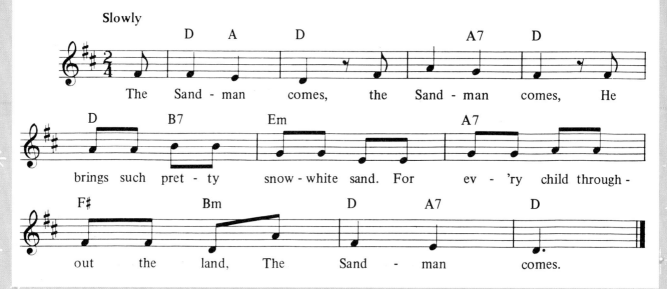

Slowly

The Sand - man comes, the Sand - man comes, He

brings such pret - ty snow - white sand. For ev - 'ry child through -

out the land, The Sand - man comes.